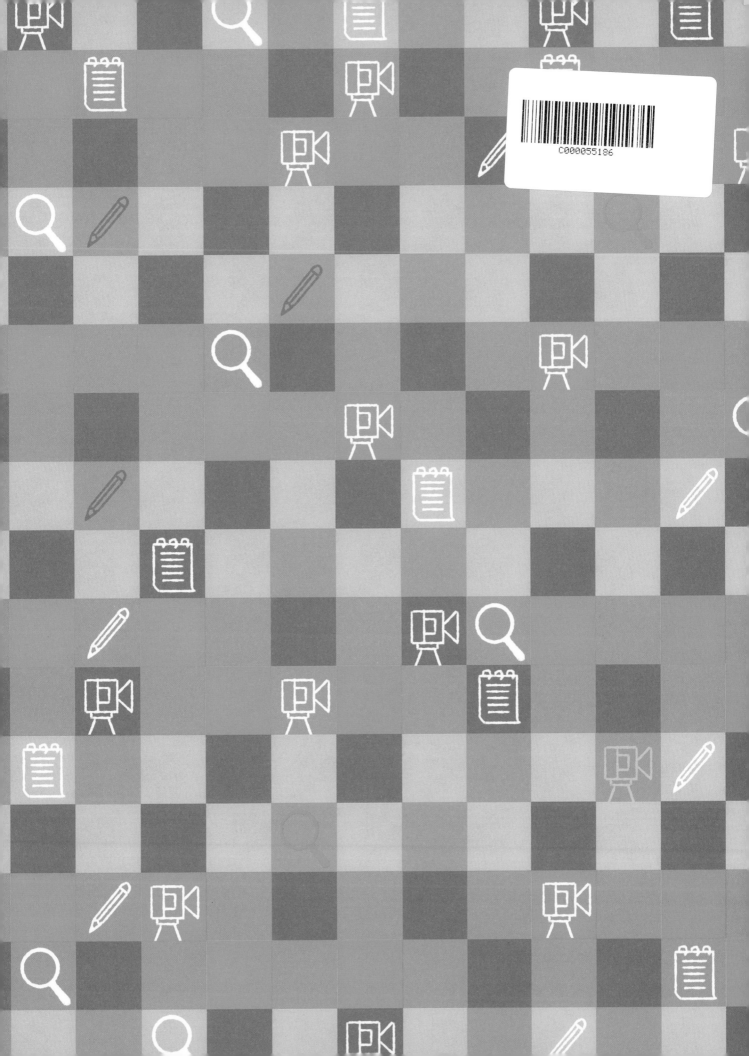

This book couldn't have been achieved without the enthusiasm and support of colleagues at ITN. Thank you to everyone from ITV News, Channel 4 News, 5 News, News Production, ITN Education and our fantastic technical teams who shared their experiences, thoughts and expertise so readily. Thanks in particular to Lisa Campbell at ITN for getting the project off the ground and for being a constant creative sounding board.

And, finally, thank you to Rachael Roberts, who edited with insight and style, and everyone at Templar for sharing our strong belief in the importance of helping young people understand and engage with how the news is made.

A TEMPLAR BOOK

First published in the UK in 2024 by Templar Books,
an imprint of Bonnier Books UK
4th Floor, Victoria House,
Bloomsbury Square, London WC1B 4DA
Owned by Bonnier Books
Sveavägen 56, Stockholm, Sweden
www.bonnierbooks.co.uk

Text copyright © 2024 by Independent Television News Limited
Illustration copyright © 2024 by Terri Po
Design copyright © 2024 by Templar Books

1 3 5 7 9 10 8 6 4 2

ISBN 978-1-80078-259-4

This book was typeset in Sofia Pro, BD Supper and Gambado Sans
The illustrations were created digitally

Written by Jane Marlow
Edited by Rachael Roberts
Designed by Chris Stanley and Adam Allori
Production by Neil Randles

Printed in China

HOW THE NEWS WORKS

WRITTEN BY
JANE MARLOW

ILLUSTRATED BY
TERRI PO

templar
books

CONTENTS

WELCOME TO THE NEWS

As a kid, news was really important to me. But when I was growing up, the internet didn't exist. Yes, I don't seem that old, but the internet isn't that old either! The only ways to stay up to date were to watch the TV news at a particular time of day, listen to the bulletins on the radio or wander to the shops to grab a newspaper. My dad even used the newspaper headlines to teach me to read and I loved it! I loved learning about what was happening in and outside of my little South London world. I decided I wanted to be the person who told those news stories too.

Being the child of a postman and social worker meant that it was going to take lots of hard work to get into the industry. No one in my family worked in media, and there were only two Black newsreaders on TV at the time. But my Jamaican-born parents taught me that no barrier could ever stop me from doing what I wanted to do. I knew it was going to be a battle, but I was prepared to fight for it.

When I finally got through the newsroom door, it was like this magical place. My days became filled with endless research, learning numerous facts, getting to the bottom of a story and then finding the right words to report it to people across the country. Now as a journalist and newsreader, I get to talk to strangers every day and help them tell their stories to the world. For me, it's an exciting – and important – thing to do. I think I've got the best job in the world. And maybe you feel the same...

Do you ever find yourself buzzing to tell a mate about the latest gossip from school, your thoughts on a new album or your predictions of the plot in your favourite show? Well, that makes you a journalist too. Or maybe you prefer to research or gather facts and figures, or constantly find yourself behind the phone camera – all these things are important when it comes to making news, and if you read on, you might be inspired to get involved yourself.

So here's what I'm going to do: myself and some other journalists are going take you on a trip of the news industry. You'll see what we do, how we put news together, what it's for and why it's important. We'll show you how to spot fake news and so much more, and maybe you'll leave wanting to be a real journalist, too. I hope you enjoy the tour!

Charlene White

Broadcaster, journalist and presenter

WHAT IS NEWS?

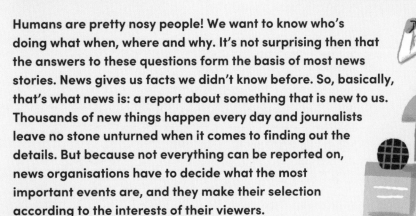

Humans are pretty nosy people! We want to know who's doing what when, where and why. It's not surprising then that the answers to these questions form the basis of most news stories. News gives us facts we didn't know before. So, basically, that's what news is: a report about something that is new to us. Thousands of new things happen every day and journalists leave no stone unturned when it comes to finding out the details. But because not everything can be reported on, news organisations have to decide what the most important events are, and they make their selection according to the interests of their viewers.

What makes something newsworthy?

Let's say a report comes in that Nora has bought a red toothbrush. That might be news, but it's not really very interesting to anyone but Nora. However, let's say you found out that Nora had invented a red toothbrush that plays a tune while you brush your teeth. Now, that is something that might get onto a newsfeed that is followed by parents, dentists and music lovers everywhere. The kind of stories that tend to make it onto the feeds of big news organisations are ones that affect lots of people's lives.

Different news for different places

LOCAL NEWS
Sometimes news stories are about things happening near you, like traffic incidents, new building projects and community events. This is local news and it's useful as it keeps us connected with people and events that happen in our area.

NATIONAL NEWS
Some news affects the whole country, so it's called national news. If the French government decides to change the school curriculum, for example, it would be important to people in France, but probably not as important to people living elsewhere. National news helps people find out about the country they live in.

INTERNATIONAL NEWS
Serious events such as wars, natural disasters or disease outbreaks might not happen near you, but they can still have an impact on your life. These stories will make it onto newsfeeds all over the world. This is known as international news. This type of news also covers issues like climate change that affect lots of countries at the same time. News providers might only report one type of news, or they might offer a whole mix, depending on their audience.

How news comes to us

TELEVISION
On TV, news is delivered through programmes shown at the same time every day. You can also watch them online or on catch-up.

WEBSITES
Many TV news organisations also have their own news websites but there are others that only exist online. Websites have a mix of video, text and audio reports, and have the space to give us more detail about a story we've seen elsewhere.

SOCIAL MEDIA
Just as friends share their news on their feeds, celebrities, influencers, organisations and even news reporters talk directly to their followers on these platforms too. They give us a person's lived experience of news and events that often takes us behind the scenes, making us feel like we have a personal connection.

RADIO AND PODCASTS
These platforms make news without any pictures, so reporters describe the news to bring it to life. Both podcasts and radio are great places to find out more detail about a story in longer reports and analysis.

NEWSPAPERS
Newspapers run the most important story on the front page with a big headline and other topics are grouped together into sections inside. Some focus on local news, whereas others cover national and international news. You can buy a print version but often their content is also published online.

WORD OF MOUTH
Whether it's face to face or messaging online, even chatting is news!

HISTORY OF THE NEWS

The need to share news has been around since humans have been on Earth. Imagine a prehistoric person spotting a hungry sabre-toothed tiger heading towards their settlement – they would have wanted to spread that news, and fast! Although news isn't always life or death, throughout history we have always wanted to hear what's happening in the world around us. More than that, we have always wanted to know it first. The competition to get the news out faster and to more and more people has driven the development of the news industry. Today, digital technology can deliver news to our phones, computers and other devices at top speed – hear it, post it, read it, share it. But it hasn't always been like that.

Ancient messengers

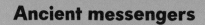

MESSENGER RUNS 50 KILOMETRES TO DELIVER NOTE

In early societies like the ancient Greeks, Egyptians and the Incas in Peru, messengers were like modern-day reporters. They travelled all over the country on foot or on horseback to deliver important messages. They had to be fit, trustworthy and able to read, write and speak many languages. Finally, they had to be brave as they might be blamed for delivering bad news, which could even lead to them being imprisoned!

SAILOR DELIVERS NEWS OF FAR-OFF LAND

Sailors also shared news about foreign countries they had visited. It wasn't their main job, but they told people in markets, bars and docks about the places, people and events they'd seen overseas. Word of mouth was a good way to spread the news, but it was important to remember the information was only as trustworthy as the person who delivered it.

Coming through! Message for the emperor!

TIMELINE

Written notices

59 BCE – NEWSPAPER PUBLISHED IN ANCIENT ROME

In ancient Rome, *Acta Diurna* was published daily in very small quantities and displayed throughout the Italian city so the citizens who knew how to read could find out the city's news. In China, a *Dibao* is an example of another ancient newspaper sharing news about the ruling family. It's hard to pinpoint the first edition, but they are thought to have been around as early as 618 CE.

Town criers

1066 – TOWN CRIER ANNOUNCES FRENCH INVASION

A town crier is someone who would stand in the town centre and signal that they had news to share by using a musical instrument to attract attention. In the UK, criers used a handbell. In the Netherlands, it was a gong, and in France and Sri Lanka, they used a drum. People knew the noise meant something important was happening – like an invasion – so would gather to hear the crier shout the news at the top of their voice.

Invaders approaching!

Printing press

1605 – THE FIRST OFFICIAL PAPER IS PRINTED IN STRASBOURG, FRANCE

When Johannes Gutenberg designed a printing press that could produce identical documents quickly and easily, he changed news forever. Not long after its invention, the first newspaper, *Relation*, was printed. It was easy to carry and share, which meant the news it contained travelled further afield. Unfortunately, not many people could read at the time, so the real benefit of the printing press was only felt when education became more accessible.

Making waves on the radio

1901 – RADIO TRANSMISSION CROSSES THE ATLANTIC

In 1901, Guglielmo Marconi broadcast the first radio transmission across the Atlantic. It was a total game-changer – this new tech sped up the spread of information at home and overseas. Then, in 1922, the British Broadcasting Corporation (BBC) was created. This was another 'wow' moment – its radio programmes were like having a turbo-charged town crier, and suddenly news could reach remote communities and even cross continents.

Too bad I can't read yet!

Global news in your living room

1967 – SATELLITE TECHNOLOGY BRINGS VIEWERS TO WHERE NEWS IS HAPPENING

In the UK, ITN's *News at Ten* shook up the TV news format by introducing the 'reporter package'. Instead of the presenter reading all the reports, satellite technology meant filmed reports from locations around the world could be on air back home within hours rather than days. Nowadays, these reports are typical all over the world.

Non-stop news

1980 – CNN IN THE US BECOMES THE FIRST 24-HOUR NEWS CHANNEL

Traditionally, TV news bulletins were broadcast at specific times throughout the day. But on 1 June 1980, the Cable News Network (CNN) began providing non-stop news all day and night. This was called 'rolling news' because there was no beginning or end and news stories could air as soon as they happened. This is known as 'breaking news'. Rolling news channels started springing up around the world, and news was delivered increasingly faster.

Sound and images become TV

1954 – THE BBC LAUNCHES ITS FIRST TELEVISION NEWS PROGRAMME

Scottish inventor John Logie Baird's thrilling television technology combined sound and moving images that drew the viewer into the heart of the action. The trailblazing BBC jumped at the chance to use clips to bring news to life in viewers' homes on TV.

Creating news personalities

1955 – ITN IS CREATED AND DEVELOPS A LESS FORMAL STYLE OF NEWS

The traditional way of delivering TV news was sometimes considered to be formal as it was done using newsreel footage and voiceover. When the organisation Independent Television News (ITN) was created, its on-screen presenters had a more casual and authentic connection with viewers. This style of newscaster was easier to relate to, and they popped up on TV news all over the world.

The World Wide Web

1989 – NEWS DISTRIBUTION REACHES WARP SPEED WHEN THE WORLD WIDE WEB IS INVENTED

Ever wondered what the 'www' stands for at the beginning of a website address? Well, it's short for the world wide web, which was invented by British computer scientist Tim Berners-Lee. We just call it the internet now but back then, his new way of sharing information was a stunning innovation that allowed news organisations to reach global audiences online without having to wait to air a report in what's known as a 'scheduled bulletin'.

Social media

2005 – VIDEO SHARING SITES MEAN ANYONE CAN BE A REPORTER

Social media rewrote the rules on who could share news and get their voice heard. News providers found a new platform to reach their audiences, but it also meant ordinary people could post and tag reporters with eyewitness accounts of newsworthy events. Social media platforms also made it easy to share or forward information quickly, again and again, from different accounts. News could be shared pretty much the moment it happened.

NEWS YOU CAN TRUST?

The word 'impartial' comes up a lot when talking about news you can trust. It's a big word that simply means the reporter or newsreader delivering the news doesn't take sides or share their own opinions in a report. An impartial news story only presents the facts so people can decide what they think.

ASK ME ANYTHING

WHAT HAPPENS DURING A REPORT ABOUT SOMETHING BAD, LIKE A CRIME? SURELY, IT'S OKAY FOR THE REPORTER TO SAY WHAT THEY THINK THEN?

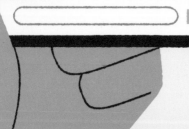

Nope. Sorry! Reporters still have to be impartial even if they feel strongly about a story. People who are interviewed as part of the report are allowed to say what they think, but not the news reporter themselves. When you're experienced, it comes naturally to let interviewees present their opinions so viewers can make up their own mind.

Balancing act

A good way to spot an impartial news report is to see if the journalist shows at least two opposing sides to a story. This is a good indicator that the news is balanced.

Let's say a reporter discovers that a brand of eco-friendly trainers is actually using unrecycled plastic to make them. In a balanced news report, the journalist would present the evidence they've gathered to prove this claim, as well as the reasons why the evidence is reliable. Then they would contact the brand to ask if they wanted to respond. By including the evidence and the brand's response, the report would be balanced.

Right to reply

A report can still be balanced even if the opposing side doesn't want to share their view. Being offered the chance to respond is called the 'right to reply' and by reporting that the person chose to turn down that opportunity, the news report can still be considered balanced and impartial.

The regulator

If a news organisation says its content is impartial, fair and balanced, it has to follow a strict set of rules that apply to all the news it produces across all its platforms. In some countries, it's against the law to break them, which means they need to be monitored.

Just like it's a superhero's job to keep people safe from wrong-doers, the regulator's job is to keep news audiences safe by making sure the news organisations it oversees stick to the rules. It's really serious stuff. If the regulator finds even a single news report that breaks the rules around impartiality, fairness and balance, a news organisation can get fined!

ON ASSIGNMENT
NEWSPAPERS VS. BROADCAST NEWS VS. ONLINE NEWS

Take a look at these students' blog posts. Both have written about how their school served an unusually large amount of carrots one lunchtime. Which post do you think is impartial and balanced?

CRUNCH TIME FOR STARVING STUDENTS
BY JING

Hundreds of children will go hungry today as teachers decided to serve ONLY CARROTS at lunchtime. It's mad – nobody likes carrots. They're disgusting.

"The horrible hairy bits on the outside creep me out," said one student. "I wouldn't eat one if they were the last vegetable on Earth."

TWO-THIRDS OF STUDENTS CHOOSE CARROTS
BY FERNANDO

The decision to serve extra carrots for school dinner today received a mixed response among students.

One carrot-loving student was thrilled. "I just love the taste," he said. "They're off-the-scale good for you too."

Another student said they did not eat carrots as the "hairy bits" on the outside gave them "the creeps".

The canteen staff told teachers that 66% of students ate the carrots, so this is being seen as a success.

13

Different rules for different countries

Every country in the world has its own rules and laws about who can publish news and what they can say, so the laws in some countries might be more lenient than others. Some countries might not insist that their news has to be impartial, which is why it's important to know whether the news you're getting is balanced or if it supports a specific a point of view.

ASK ME ANYTHING

IS IT ALWAYS WRONG FOR NEWS ORGANISATIONS TO HAVE AN OPINION?

Not necessarily – as long as you know what that opinion is. But this might take a bit of investigating as it's not always obvious. There's a place for opinionated news but it needs to be clear that a report or feature is commenting on a story rather than reporting it.

Making your mind up

Hearing a range of views about a topic can often help you form your own opinions. Sometimes it's easy to know what you think about things. Do you like strawberries? No. Do you think koalas are cute? Yes. Do you like going on holiday? Absolutely!

Other times, questions are more complicated and it's important to have as much information as possible before making your mind up. Is nuclear power good or bad? Should school exams be banned? Should 16-year-olds be allowed to vote?

The news often looks at these trickier questions, so it's essential to know if a news platform has a specific opinion about the issues they're covering. That way you can work out if you're only hearing one side of a story or if you need to look elsewhere to find a balanced view.

It's my way or the highway!

Some news organisations make commitments to produce news that is impartial. Some examples are ITN, the BBC and the Associated Press. These values apply to all their platforms; whether you go to their social media pages, websites or watch them on TV, their content follows the same standards and rules.

But news platforms that aren't impartial can sometimes support the views of the person who owns them. Let's say a news organisation is owned by someone who makes lots of money from selling lemonade. It might not be in its interest to write reports that criticise lemonade, even if they are true. In fact, it could be more likely to report news that shows lemonade in a good light and only criticises other fizzy drinks.

Another big influence on news is politics. Just like the lemonade seller, news platforms might only publish positive news about a political group their owner supports and leave out negative facts and opinions. It's really important to make an informed decision on big topics like this, so it's a good idea to find another platform that reports the other side of the story too, or one that covers both.

NEWS ALERT
WHAT IS CLICKBAIT?

Clickbait describes a headline that is so outrageous or tempting that it makes you click through to read the whole story. The more clicks or views this content gets, the more money the owner makes from advertisers. They might look like real news stories but a headline about a celebrity that sounds a bit bonkers should trigger a warning to think more deeply about whether the story is true. Think about whether you want these stories to make more money through your clicks!

SCIENTISTS DON'T WANT YOU TO KNOW THIS ONE WEIRD TRICK

FLYING PIG SIGHTED

ON ASSIGNMENT
NEWSPAPERS VS. BROADCAST NEWS VS. ONLINE NEWS

Find three versions of the same news story: one from a news organisation you know and trust, one from a news website you don't know and another in a print or online newspaper. Can you work out if they are fair and balanced or whether they have a specific point of view?

WHAT IS FAKE NEWS?

The most important thing about the news is that it's trustworthy. But what about when it's not? Fake news is exactly that – news stories that are false. Whether inaccurate stories are reported accidently or on purpose, they can have harmful consequences. Fake news can make you believe things that are untrue and might even make you change your opinion based on false information. Even worse, it can lead you to mistrust all news.

Don't believe the lies!

Fake news is dangerous because it can make you believe things that aren't true. Have a look at this situation and see if you can spot the sneaky ways it can trick you into believing lies. Look out for the ways fake news tries to look real, how it uses unreliable sources and how it exploits emotions and fears.

How fake news creates mistrust

Not only can fake news make you believe in lies, but over time, it can lead to you mistrusting news as a whole. How does this work? Let's look at a scenario...

Imagine Aisha invites you to her party. Result! Aisha's parties are great and last year you had a blast feeding llamas at the farm. Later, your friend Adam says that everyone at Aisha's party will go in a hot-air balloon. Amazing! You share the news with everyone and get super excited, but when you arrive at Aisha's party, there is no hot-air balloon. It's just a regular party. You end up feeling disappointed and will probably think twice about believing Adam again.

Fake news has the same effect, but false reports about important topics can have more serious consequences than a party going from amazing to meh. If you believe a news report and later discover the information it provided was untrue, you may think twice about trusting that news organisation again. While questioning news organisations that provide unreliable information is an important skill, it becomes a problem if the experience leads you to mistrusting other news providers. You might start to question whether you can trust any at all, leading you to doubt factual and reliable news.

Types of fake news

Not all fake news is the same. This is because there are different ways that false information can be reported. While all fake news is harmful, it's not always intentional. There are two main types of fake news and it's important to know the difference between them.

DISINFORMATION is when someone lies on purpose. For example, if Adam had deliberately made up the story about the hot-air balloon to try and create a bad atmosphere at Aisha's party.

MISINFORMATION is when someone gets their facts wrong by mistake, like if Adam had genuinely believed there would be a hot-air balloon at Aisha's party but he turned out to be mistaken.

NEWS ALERT
FAKE NEWS OR FALSE ALARM?

Sometimes people use the phrase 'fake news' to describe a fact or a news story they don't agree with, even if it's definitely true. This is still harmful as people could end up believing them and not checking the facts for themselves.

WELCOME TO THE NEWSROOM

You've probably seen news stories written as articles online or maybe in newspapers. Well, TV news works in a similar way. It's a selection of the most important news stories of the day but instead of being published as something to read, they're grouped into programmes called news bulletins that are broadcast live at the same time every day. Let's take a tour around the newsroom to see how things are done.

Meet our newsreader

When you watch a news bulletin, you'll spot someone who guides you through the reports. That person is called the newsreader, and today that is me! I'm going to show you what happens as we prepare to broadcast live.

Live bulletins spark a buzz in the studio. In front of me are the cameras, camera operators and the studio floor manager. Through my earpiece, the production assistant counts down the seconds until we're live.

1. With seconds to go, I do a final run through of the programme in my head. Each story can affect a viewer in a different way – it can teach them something they didn't know before and it can be both informative and emotional. The biggest part of my job is to make sure the viewer understands and trusts the news I'm delivering is impartial and fair, so how I say my words is very important.

Live in 30 seconds...

2. My prep has been done before I even step into the studio. I've written my headlines, researched the reports that will be aired and looked over the questions I'll ask our news correspondents and guests. I've also read the scripts aloud to make sure they're correct and sound like me.

20 seconds...

ON ASSIGNMENT
BE A PRESENTER

Newsreaders wear an earpiece while presenting so the director, producer and production assistant can give them instructions, updates and information during the bulletin. Throughout all this, the newsreader must keep presenting without stopping, pausing or looking confused.

How about giving it a go? Get a friend to talk to you on the phone while you read a news report out loud and see how you get on. It's harder than it looks!

A newsreader's day: behind the scenes!

Presenting the news is so much more than just reading the bulletins. Follow the timeline below to see what a newsreader does throughout the day.

12.00 – Arrive at the newsroom.

14.30 – Meet with the news team and decide which stories will be featured.

15:30 – Get dressed for the show.

16:30 – Work with the programme editor to write the headlines.

17:00 – Read and edit the script for the bulletin to suit the newsreader's voice.

18:15 – Arrive at the studio.

18:20 – Fit and check the earpiece to make sure it works.

18:30 – Go live on air!

3. When I reach the studio, the scripts have already been loaded onto the autocue, but I also have a paper copy on my desk. Using paper is old-school, but it's a lifesaver if any of the tech breaks down!

10 seconds...

4. The opening tune starts to play and I take a deep breath. Then I hear the director's voice in my earpiece:

Cue headlines.

And we're off! As I look into the camera, I feel like I'm talking directly to you. In my head, I'm on your sofa with you telling you a story.

And that's not all...

The newsreader might be who you see on screen, but they're just one member of a huge team that creates the bulletin and gets the programme on TV. So, let's meet the journalists, editors, producers, tech operators and everyone else who brings the news to our screens!

WHO'S WHO IN THE NEWS PROCESS

Editors

Lots of news happens all over the world every day, but it would be impossible to include every single story. That's why there are editors to decide which stories will be reported. Whether they work in the TV newsroom, for a print newspaper or news website, it's the editor's job to pick the most interesting story for their audience. Here are a few that work in my newsroom.

Each bulletin has a **PROGRAMME EDITOR**. They work with all the reporters and editors to develop their news stories, then they decide which ones will go on air.

SPECIALIST EDITORS focus on finding stories about specific topics like entertainment, sports or politics. They work on their stories with the **HOME NEWS EDITOR** if it's about something in their country, or the **FOREIGN NEWS EDITOR** if the story is about something happening abroad.

DIGITAL EDITORS create short reports called explainers, blogs and special bulletins that are designed specifically for online platforms. They also cut down reports made for the TV bulletin and put them online and on social media.

On the road team

Often journalists work on their reports in the newsroom, but the on the road team are the people who leave the newsroom to report the news wherever it's happening, at home or abroad.

REPORTERS go out and find news stories and when they think they've found something interesting, they tell an editor. If the editor is interested in the story and believes it will appeal to their audience, the newsgathering process kicks off. The reporters research the story by finding out facts and interviewing people to hear their views.

CAMERA OPERATORS decide what images will help tell the news story in the most engaging way possible. They have to position their camera in a good spot for static interviews, find the best angles for interview close-ups and shots to set the scene, and be ready to film on the move.

PRODUCERS are journalists too, but they work behind the camera. They help the reporter with research, securing interviews and fact-checking, and they make sure the whole process – including filming the report – runs smoothly.

There's also another kind of editor who creates the report using the footage the camera operator has filmed. To distinguish them from the newsroom editors, we call them the **PICTURE EDITOR**. They use editing software to cut the footage together to create a video report.

GRAPHIC DESIGNERS are part of the technology team too. They produce exciting visuals like graphs and explainers that pop up on screen during a news report to make information easier to understand.

In the studio

The cameras in the studio are much bigger than the ones used on location. They are mounted on a base with smooth wheels so they can glide silently across the studio. The **STUDIO CAMERA OPERATOR** makes sure their camera is in the right position at the right time to produce steady, in-focus shots of the newsreader and guests.

The **LIGHTING DIRECTOR'S** role is to position lights on the set so that viewers see an accurate image of the people in the studio. That might mean adding more lights for people with darker skin or soft lights for people with blonde hair. During the bulletin, they use a console in the gallery to adjust the lights to achieve the look the director wants.

The **FLOOR MANAGER** is the director's eyes in the studio. They relay information from the director to the newsreader and the rest of the studio crew. They also set up everyone's microphones and make sure guests get on and off the set at the right times.

In the gallery

When a news bulletin airs live, a group of people are hard at work behind the scenes controlling which images and sounds are seen and heard. They do this in a room called the gallery. In here, a huge dashboard is connected to all the studio cameras and news feeds coming from the reporters scheduled to be part of the bulletin.

WASPS VOTE TO STRIKE AFTER SOFT DRINKS TAX ANNOUNCED

NASA PLANS TO UPGRADE MOON TO LED

DINOSAUR BONES FOUND AT LOCH NESS

ANNUAL HOTDOG CONTEST CANCELLED DUE TO SAUSAGE SHORTAGE

The **PRODUCTION ASSISTANT** (or PA) makes sure the bulletin starts and ends on time. A scheduled TV bulletin has to be a precise length, so they tell the director and newsreader if the bulletin is running too short or too long so the pace can be adjusted.

The **VISION MIXER** uses the buttons on the dashboard to cut between the incoming feeds from the different cameras in the studio and on location. These choices become the sounds, graphics and images that appear live on air.

The **DIRECTOR** is like the captain of a spaceship and is in control of what goes on air. They talk to their team in the gallery, the newsreader and the reporters about what's coming up in the bulletin. They also make snappy decisions if something in the bulletin needs to change super-fast.

TYPES OF NEWS

You've probably noticed that not all news is about the same thing. Some topics feature very often, like sport, politics and entertainment, and others less so. But why is this? Well, different topics might be more urgent or have a greater effect on our lives, or even just be more popular. Many stories are newsworthy, but news organisations need to strike a balance between what people need and want to see. It's important for reporters to have detailed knowledge about a specific topic to explain stories accurately. That's why many reporters choose an area to develop as their specialism.

Becoming a correspondent

Finding a specialism works a lot like school. A journalist starts off as a 'general reporter' and learns the basics about a range of subjects. When they find a topic they're passionate about, they'll study and research it in depth. Finally, if a journalist is given a specialist role in a newsroom, they become a correspondent.

Making good contacts

Having a specialism helps journalists get exclusive stories. By focussing on one area of reporting, journalists build strong relationships with important people in that field. These people are called contacts. If a journalist wants to verify a piece of information in a story they're working on, they can reach out to their contacts and ask for an opinion. The more a contact gets to know and trust a journalist, the more likely they are to share insider information, and the more accurate and reliable information they give, the more confidence the journalist will have in them.

ASK ME ANYTHING

WHAT'S AN ANONYMOUS SOURCE?

Sometimes a contact might give information but won't want people to know it came from them. We say this information has been given to a journalist 'off the record'. When this happens, a reporter can use that information as background research for their report, or they can quote the person's words as coming from an anonymous source. 'On the record' means a contact is happy for their name to be used alongside their comments.

---

8 A.M. HEADLINES

1. Scientist found safe after solo mission to reach the North Pole

2. Government faces strong challenge in today's general election

Check back later for more news updates

Finding the news you want

News is fast, unpredictable and constantly changing, so organising it into sections and topics also helps us find the reports we're interested in. A scheduled TV bulletin has limited time so instead of arranging news into sections, it jumps from topic to topic, focussing on the stories the editor decides are most important. Newspapers have sections but they generally only publish once a day, meaning they can't provide updates or breaking news. But don't worry! Online news platforms have this covered.

Look at the news website to the left to see how reports get organised into subject tabs as stories develop or as more pressing news breaks. Start with the 8 a.m. headlines and follow the arrows throughout the day.

---

1 P.M. HEADLINES

1. Government faces strong challenge in today's general election

2. Chaos as AI robots in school canteen give students the wrong food

SCIENCE

10 P.M. HEADLINES

1. Government suffers heavy defeat in general election

2. Ash cloud created by volcanic eruption disrupts travel

SCIENCE

POLITICS

SPORTS NEWS

Sports reporting attracts audiences to news platforms as it's such a popular topic – millions of people all over the world follow hundreds of different sports. Reporting the most exciting and interesting news is key. As well as being fun, top level sports are big businesses and changes can affect the wider world. There's lots to cover with this topic, so let's dive in!

What is sports news?

There's more to sports news than just reporting results. Audiences expect to hear expert views about the background to each event, athletes' performance statistics and even result predictions. Correspondents gather facts and statistics from official sources to use in their reports. Interviews with athletes, coaches and sports organisations are another big part of sports news, so reporters need good contacts to help them set up interviews and hopefully get exclusives.

Sports and the bigger picture

Sports news isn't limited to games and matches – it can cross over into other topics too. If a local football club at the heart of a community closes, people will lose their jobs and local business will miss out on the money sports fans bring in. This then becomes a business story too.

On a larger scale, accusations of cheating in a certain sport might lead to a serious investigation into that sport's culture and whether it's run fairly. International sports tournaments can even make headlines if there are issues surrounding the host country, such as having a poor record on human rights. Reports on the event might incorporate a political angle, such as discussions about where people stand on the issue and whether sportswashing is happening.

ASK ME ANYTHING

WHAT IS SPORTSWASHING?

Sportswashing is when a country, company or individual uses the positivity of a sports event to distract people from something undesirable they've done.

Sports coverage in action

Buckle-up! We're heading to one of the world's biggest sporting events – the Summer Olympics – to find out how sports reporting happens. Read each section to see how it's done.

ACCESS ALL AREAS

First, a news organisation will apply for press passes. These passes give the news crew permission to access the stadiums and all of the rooms and facilities provided specifically for the media.

THE PRESS ROOM

This is the hub where reporters and news crews can work on their reports and scripts, and sports associations and event organisers can share information with news crews easily. Here, the room is buzzing with reporters working to deadlines and competing for exclusives to make their news stories stand out. At big events, there are often screens that show all the events happening at once so reporters can keep up with the action as they're working to a deadline. Press conferences are also held in the press room after an event. Journalists gather to ask athletes questions about their performance and the result.

ON SITE

Sports reporting also happens on location. Reporters talk to a news camera that's connected to an outside broadcast (OB) van. The broadcast is beamed up to a satellite, then down to a server in the newsroom that connects to the gallery. The report is then broadcast from the gallery to your TV.

Hitting the deadline

TV news reports must be ready for a specific time, which can lead to some tricky situations when it comes to sport reporting. Imagine a team is moments away from reaching the Olympic volleyball final, but the bulletin is about to air and there's no result to report. What happens now? The reporter must pivot! They'll summarise the match so far and how the team is playing, and maybe speak to an expert to predict the result. The news team can create a follow-up report when the match has finished, to be posted online or in the next bulletin.

FOREIGN NEWS

Foreign news covers everything newsworthy that happens outside your home country. Knowing what's happening across the world is important because we are all connected through things like trade, politics, science, medicine and climate change. Events on the other side of the world can affect you even if you're not there, so news reporters called foreign correspondents travel around the world to make sure we stay up-to-date with breaking news that's happening elsewhere.

What makes foreign news newsworthy?

Lots of events around the world have importance on a global scale. These can be planned and predictable things, like national elections or conferences attended by world leaders about important issues, but there are also sudden and shocking events that can shake the world in an instant. Natural disasters often have wide-reaching effects, and countries need support from the whole world to get on their feet again. Scientific discoveries like new vaccines or computer technology can change how the world operates forever.

Working abroad

Because foreign news is such a big subject (and the world is such a big place!), some correspondents are based in other countries for months or even years at permanent offices called bureaus. The countries they go to are often ones that have a longstanding relationship with their home country. These correspondents have in-depth knowledge of the country they are based in, and report political, cultural and environmental news, as well as anything else that happens there that affects audiences back home.

What's it like where you are?

War reporting

One of the most dangerous situations a correspondent can report from is a war zone. It's important work because we rely on reporters sharing their first-hand knowledge of conflicts to help us understand what's happening. Finding out the background to the conflict, how it affects the nations that are involved and even the ones that aren't is important information for people around the world. Let's look at how this dangerous job is done...

War reporting feels like you're walking towards danger while everyone else is running away. Every day is unpredictable, and situations can go from calm to unsafe really quickly. The news organisation discusses every detail of an assignment to make sure it can keep its news team safe. Here are some measures they take:

- News organisations provide safe accommodation for their teams.

- News teams are paired with friendly armed forces to help them travel safely around the war zone.

- News teams are given special equipment such as biohazard suits, flak jackets, armoured vehicles, helmets, plus reinforced tech to send their reports back to the newsroom.

- News teams are given large labels and badges marked 'PRESS', making it clear that they are journalists, not soldiers or spies.

- War reporters are given regular health and safety updates so they know how to stay safe.

ASK ME ANYTHING

HOW DO JOURNALISTS WORK WITH THE ARMY?

When a reporter travels with an army unit, we call this 'being embedded'. Whilst there, they give viewers a close-up view of the conditions of war and also explain what the soldiers are doing. Even though reporters get to know the soldiers they're travelling with, their reports must always be fair and factual.

ON ASSIGNMENT
NEWS OR PROPAGANDA

Balanced news helps us work out our view about an event or situation. Propaganda is the opposite of balanced news because it promotes only one point of view. It's often used in wars to inspire people to support one side of the conflict. Propaganda might be a poster or video or message, but in each case, it's designed to make you believe the message it's presenting while concealing the whole truth.

Look at these two posters and decide which is news and which is propaganda.

Badgers are cute and cuddly and can do no wrong.

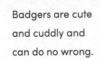

Badgers are playful animals, but can also spread disease that is harmful to cattle.

ENTERTAINMENT NEWS

Entertainment news is all about celebrities, film, music, art – in fact, everything to do with popular culture. People around the world want to find out about entertainers they admire and the exciting projects they're working on. For that reason, entertainment reporters focus on getting exclusive information about upcoming events and access to the biggest stars in the business.

How do we get entertainment news?

Entertainment news can come at the drop of a hat – a film studio might unveil a new trailer, a band might release a song or a TV show line-up might be announced. But while celebrities and entertainers are doing things constantly, that doesn't always mean there's news.

Award ceremonies, fashion shows and festivals are part of something called the entertainment 'diary'. These are events that come around at fixed times every year and are hotspots for news. Journalists set up interviews with attending celebrities in advance to get the latest scoop, and produce 'off diary' stories based on their observations at the event.

Offering expert analysis

An important part of a correspondent's job is to report their expert opinion on the latest entertainment. In this situation, opinions are fine as they are clearly labelled as a review. Of course celebrities will want to promote their new movie or play, book or music album, which is why it's important for entertainment correspondents to offer their opinion and help audiences make up their own minds. In newspapers and magazines, you will often see stars alongside their review. Five stars means something's amazing! But if there's only one star, maybe give it a miss...

Getting the best celebrity interview

Celebrity interviews are one of the best parts of the job, but the trick is to find a fresh angle to make your report stand out. Film star Maisie Minestrone is coming to town to promote her latest film, so here's how an entertainment correspondent makes sure their interview is the one everyone wants to watch.

1. GETTING THE INTERVIEW

Celebrities like Maisie are often represented by a public relations (PR) company, which helps manage their image and reputation. The correspondent contacts Maisie's PR team and they agree that an interview on their news platform would be a great opportunity. Maisie is doing one day of back-to-back interviews and the correspondent is given a slot at 5 p.m. Result!

2. RESEARCH TIME

To find out as much as they can about her background and work, the correspondent reads previous interviews with Maisie. Next, they write up their questions, but before diving into the serious stuff, the correspondent will open with a friendly question to build a connection and make Maisie feel relaxed, like a question about Maisie's pink hair or Polly, her pet python.

3. WORKING WITH THE PR TEAM

On the day of the interview, the correspondent, producer and camera operator work with Maisie's team to set up. The PR team says questions about Maisie's hair colour and pet python Polly are off limits. If the correspondent doesn't respect this request, Maisie's PR team won't allow them interviews in future, so they have to find a new icebreaker fast.

4. MAKING IT A SUCCESS

It's time for the interview and the correspondent remembers from their research that Maisie loves to skateboard. Asking about Maisie's best tricks is a great icebreaker, and she relaxes as she talks about a subject she adores. Maisie mentions how she misses the freedom to go to the skatepark like she did when she was a kid. Kaboom! The correspondent now has a unique angle that will have audiences flocking to their news platform.

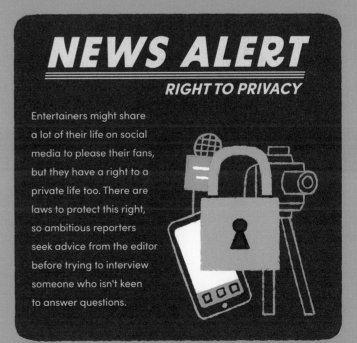

NEWS ALERT
RIGHT TO PRIVACY

Entertainers might share a lot of their life on social media to please their fans, but they have a right to a private life too. There are laws to protect this right, so ambitious reporters seek advice from the editor before trying to interview someone who isn't keen to answer questions.

INVESTIGATIONS

Investigative reports are typically TV programmes or longer news articles that report on a specific issue in detail. A reporter might uncover a lead through their own research or pick up on something that's been touched on in the news previously and believe there is more detail to be discovered. The topic under investigation could be anything, but often reports focus on crime, corruption or rule-breaking. Unlike the fast-paced daily news, some investigations – especially those involving lots of data to analyse – take place over a long period of time.

Working on an investigation

Investigative reports are very detailed so there are lots of stages to go through to make sure the information is gathered properly and all the necessary checks are done. Let's see this in action by following a reporter as they build a news story into an investigative report.

1. FINDING A LEAD

A local news station reports that a house fire started when a toaster burst into flames. It seems like a routine news story until a reporter hears about another toaster catching fire in someone else's home. When the reporter learns that both toasters were made by the same company, they think this is a story worth investigating.

2. GATHERING EVIDENCE AND CHECKING FACTS

Next, the reporter contacts the people who experienced the fires to check out the facts. They both confirm that the toaster definitely caused the fire. Suspecting there could be even more incidents, the reporter calls an organisation that handles complaints about products. The organisation shares the complaints is has recieved about the toaster and the reporter tracks down other people to hear their stories too. The more evidence, the better.

3. STARTING THE INVESTIGATION

Now that the reporter has evidence, they ask the company to respond to the information gathered. Unfortunately, the company boss doesn't want to talk about the faulty toasters, but the reporter still wants to develop the story. They decide that filming undercover at the factory is the best way to find out if the company is making unsafe products.

4. GOING UNDERCOVER

Undercover filming involves lots of resources and planning, and because there are special rules around secret filming, the editor and the news organisation's lawyers have to give their approval before it can go ahead. The reporter researches the questions that need answering for the report, and the tech team fit a recording device on the reporter before they visit the factory. Once there, the disguised reporter records evidence that supports their story, and tries to leave undetected.

5. RIGHT TO REPLY

With the footage secured, the editor and lawyers check it and confirm it is fair and accurate. Then the report is sent to the boss of the toaster company, who is given another chance to comment. The reporter gives them time to reply as they may want to put forward another side of the story, or an apology and plan to fix the problem. If the company boss replies, it's added to the report. If not, the reporter might visit the company to talk in person. Finally, the reporter waits for the deadline and finishes the report, which the editor and lawyers watch before approving it to air.

Making a difference

Investigative reporters often choose to report a story because they want to make a positive difference. They believe that the information uncovered is in the public interest, meaning it affects the well-being of regular citizens. Investigations can bring about changes in the law, expose crimes or wrong-doing or highlight injustices that some groups in society face. In our reporter's case, the investigation could lead the manufacturer to improve the safety of their toasters, preventing house fires in the future. Result!

A DAY IN THE LIFE OF A REPORTER

Now you know a bit more about the teams involved in making the news and the types of news they cover, let's see how it all works in action. Follow me as we create a report for an evening bulletin.

ASK ME ANYTHING

WHAT'S THE DIFFERENCE BETWEEN A JOURNALIST, A REPORTER AND A CORRESPONDENT?

'Journalist' is a general term for people who research and gather news, including producers, editors and reporters. But not all journalists are reporters! Reporters are people who deliver the news to the public, either on camera or in a written article, and a correspondent is a reporter who specialises in a specific topic.

First, meet Anita, our news reporter. If she's going to get a story on the news this evening, she needs to find a lead. This is a piece of information that hints there is a news story to report – a little like a detective finding a clue.

Current time
1 0 : 3 0

Bulletin airs
1 8 : 0 0

NEWS ALERT
WHERE DOES NEWS COMES FROM?

FOLLOWING A LEAD – Reporters can find a lead themselves or an editor might pass on a lead to a reporter to research.

PLANNED EVENTS – These are things we know are going to happen like conferences of world leaders, protests or film premieres.

BREAKING NEWS – These are news stories that happen unexpectedly, such as a traffic accident or even a volcano erupting.

Finding a lead

To find a lead, the first thing Anita does is check the wires. These are private websites where professional journalists from all over the world post breaking news. Anita's scrolling through the stories when her phone buzzes. She's been tagged on social media showing phone footage of a whale in a river.

Actual WHALE stranded in the river #investigate #news @reporterAnita #savethewhale now!

Gathering sources

It's a great lead, but immediately Anita's fake news klaxon goes off. Before doing anything, she needs to get a reliable source to confirm the story. A source can be a person or an organisation, so Anita contacts the river police and the coastguard to make sure the story is true.

A whale has been sighted in the river and we're working to help it get back on course.

First to post

Anita needs to work quickly. If she gets the story online first, people are more likely to stick with her news organisation for updates. With two sources confirming the story, she tells Andy, the digital editor, about her lead.

I have footage of the stranded whale. Can we put the video on our website and socials as soon as possible?

Absolutely, Anita! Send me all the information you have.

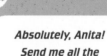

Approval to go

Next, Anita pitches the story to Beatriz, the programme editor, for the evening bulletin. Beatriz agrees that viewers will be interested, so she asks Anita to find out why the whale has gone off course and what's being done to save it. Beatriz allocates Anita's story three minutes on the evening news, and the deadline to get the report ready to air is 5.30 p.m. Brilliant! Anita has found her story and heads off to the location. She has only a few hours to create her report.

In the field

Anita arranges to meet the producer, Sania, and camera operator, Karen, at the river where the whale was last seen, to research and film the news report. This is called newsgathering, and teamwork is crucial to make it a success.

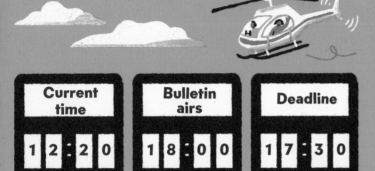

Current time	Bulletin airs	Deadline
12:20	18:00	17:30

We have less than five hours so let's decide what we need for this report.

The team works closely to prepare for the live section of the bulletin and produce the filmed section of their report. This is known as a package or VT, which is short for video tape. The VT usually includes a piece to camera, which is when the reporter talks to the viewers directly, as well as interviews and facts to help explain the information. At the end there is sometimes a live two-way, which is when the newsreader asks the reporter questions about the report.

Getting opinions

Anita spots a group of climate activists on the riverbank and goes to find out why they're there. She thinks this might be more than just a whale that has lost its way and getting their side of the story will help her create a balanced report.

Why do you think climate change has caused this whale to go off course?

Finding the facts

Sania's big job is doing the research. She finds out when the whale was first seen, if it's well and what the authorities are doing to help it back to sea. If she can get any information about the rescue exclusively, that will make the report even stronger. Sania specialises in science, so she sets up expert interviews with a zoologist to find out more about the whale's habits and a climate expert to respond to the activists' comments.

Will you give us an exclusive interview?

Shooting the images

Capturing footage of the whale is Karen's biggest challenge because it's underwater most of the time. But capturing it on camera will make the report fly! She asks the coastguard where the whale is most likely to be seen so she can make sure her camera is set up in the best spot when it surfaces.

That's a wrap

As the team pull the report together, Sania is in charge of keeping everyone working to the deadline. She organises regular catch ups to make sure things are on track. As the story takes shape, Anita starts to write the script for the VT and when the team and the programme editor are happy that the script is accurate and impartial, they send it with the footage to the picture editor and graphics team back in the newsroom.

In the edit

Making a news report is a lot like doing a jigsaw. Now that Anita, Sania and Karen have made all the pieces for the VT, the next step is putting them in the right order. To do that, they work with the graphic designer, Winston, and the picture editor, Jules, back at the newsroom.

Current time	Bulletin airs	Deadline
16:00	18:00	17:30

Preparing the graphics

Winston reads Anita's script, looking out for notes telling him what graphics are needed for the report and where they should go. There's one! Anita has written 'animate' in the margin. Graphics are really useful when there's no footage available to show an important part of the story. Winston calls Sania to discuss ideas. He needs to think quickly and creatively.

> Yes. I'll create a map showing its usual route alongside the route it took to end up in the river.

> Can we show our viewers how far the whale has gone off course?

Piecing the report together

Anita, Karen and Sania have worked hard to make an informative and balanced report, so Jules, the picture editor, has to follow the instructions in the script closely when he creates the VT. He goes through all the elements of the report: Anita's piece to camera, interviews with the public, climate activists and experts, the graphic... Wait! Where's the graphic?

Using editing software, Jules trims the clips and transitions smoothly between each shot so that the video flows according to the script. If he has an idea to add something that isn't in the script, he checks with Anita because any changes could affect the tone of the report.

Finally, Jules calls the team on location to play the VT they've made using their footage, Winston's graphics and Anita's voice over. With approval from the team, Jules sends the VT to the programme editor to be approved with minutes to spare.

NEWS ALERT
GRAPHICS

Graphics are still or animated pictures that go alongside the reporter's words to help viewers understand the report. They illustrate key points clearly and usually last up to 30 seconds. Here are some types of graphic:

MAPS
These show routes and locations, such as where the whale was spotted in the river.

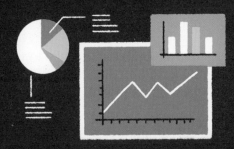

GRAPHS AND CHARTS
These are perfect for bringing facts and figures to life. Anita could use a graph to show statistics the climate expert may mention when being interviewed.

EXPLAINERS
These are pictures that help explain the report, such as an image of the whale next to a person to give viewers an idea of its size.

Going live on air

Now the report has been approved by the editor and is ready to air, it's time for me to do my bit. I go to the set and get my microphone fitted by the floor manager and settle in behind the newsdesk. The director, Ade, is in charge, and he and his team are in the gallery making sure they have all the VTs and live feeds needed for the bulletin.

Current time	Bulletin airs
17:50	18:00

Beatriz has worked with a lot of reporters – including Anita and her team – throughout the day. She's selected eight of the strongest news stories to make up the bulletin. She's checked them and is happy that they're balanced, impartial and good to air.

Beatriz gives Ade the bulletin's running order, which is a list of all the stories in the order they should appear in the programme. The most important is the headline, the report that will air first. Anita's story number is two.

Over to the director

Throughout the day, the programme editor has been in charge of the bulletin, but as soon as the news goes on air, the director is in control of the running order. The director needs to know the sequence of the news reports and which reporters will be talking live to the newsreader during the bulletin. They also need to confirm that the VTs are ready to play out, how long each report is and whether there could be any technical problems with the reporters on location.

The director has to be prepared to make clear, last-minute changes if something goes wrong. It's a high-pressure job! There can't be any pauses or blank spaces, and the programme has to keep going.

Last minute changes

Ade tells me through my earpiece that the VT for the headline story hasn't arrived, so we're going to air Anita's report first. With a last-minute change, there's no discussion – what the director says goes. I remain calm as I'm prepared and know just what to do.

As Tina, the production assistant, counts down the final seconds to the broadcast, I'm aware that the VT for the headline might come in at any minute and the story will be put back in the running order. All I can do is wait for Ade's instructions.

Live on air

The opening music plays and when I finish reading the headlines, Ade tells me to introduce Anita's report. Brilliant! Anita's VT plays without a hitch. When it finishes, Ade says to go into the interview with Anita, who is reporting from her location by the river. I ask her my follow-up questions, and the report is a huge success.

Has the coastguard told you if the whale is healthy?

Yes, Charlene. It's a bit confused no doubt, but it is doing really well.

Signing off

So that's how a report is made. It feels great to broadcast the news that the whole team - Anita, Sania, Karen, Beatriz, Winston, Jules, Ade, Tina and myself - has worked so hard to uncover. Next time you watch a news report, you'll know just how much work went into it that day.

NEWS THAT SHAPED THE WORLD

News is powerful. Through news reports, people across the globe have been able to view some of the most exceptional events in human history, and how they have inspired, ignited and changed the world.

Holding authorities to account

GANDHI BEGINS HIS SALT SATYAGRAHA

When: 12 March – 6 April 1930

Where: India

What happened? Political activist Mahatma Gandhi organised a peaceful 386-kilometre march to protest against the high tax on salt. The tax was introduced by the British Raj, and it caused hardship for Indians all over the country.

What changed? Gandhi hoped his peaceful protest, known as *satyagraha*, would gather interest around his campaign to free India from British rule. He announced to the media – print, radio and filmmakers – that at the end of the march, he would break the law by making salt out of sea water. By letting the press know his intention, he created huge anticipation and momentum around his goal. News reports were published globally, highlighting the issue and advancing the cause for Indian independence.

Connecting with people outside our community

NELSON MANDELA SENTENCED TO LIFE IN PRISON

When: 12 June 1964

Where: Johannesburg, South Africa

What happened? Activist Nelson Mandela campaigned for equal rights for all races at a time when only white people were allowed to have power in South Africa. He was arrested for trying to bring about a revolution.

What changed? Press coverage of Mandela's imprisonment and visits from journalists to his prison cell created awareness of his fight against apartheid, South Africa's system of laws that discriminated against non-white people by separating them from white communities. As a result, other countries started to support Mandela's cause and took action to stop trading with South Africa while apartheid was in place. Apartheid ended in 1990 and Mandela was released from prison.

Making the world more open

CHERNOBYL NUCLEAR DISASTER

When: 26 April 1986

Where: Chernobyl, Soviet Union (present-day Ukraine)

What happened? In April 1986, the nuclear power station in Chernobyl exploded. It was the worst nuclear disaster ever recorded and covered the town in a deadly radioactive gas that spread far over Europe.

What changed? Before the disaster, the Soviet Union was very secretive and isolated from the rest of the world. The Chernobyl disaster was so catastrophic and affected so many countries that global press outlets wanted to know what caused the explosion. As a result of the disaster, nuclear safety was seen to be a global concern. The safety issues of the Soviet Union's nuclear facilities were exposed, and its leaders were forced to be more open with the rest of the world.

Understanding other people's lives

INDIAN OCEAN EARTHQUAKE AND TSUNAMI

When: 26 December 2004

Where: Indonesia, Sri Lanka, India, Maldives and Thailand

What happened? An enormous earthquake shook the bed of the Indian Ocean, creating a series of gigantic waves that gained height and speed as they sped across the ocean. When the huge wall of water reached land, it killed 200,000 people and destroyed whole communities.

What changed? Social media wasn't around at that time, but footage shot by eyewitnesses on mobile phones was used in news reports. It was one of the most powerful examples of citizen journalism as the footage allowed people all over the world to see the scale of the disaster. Charities were set up to help the victims and donations came from people across the world.

Inspiring us to great achievements

**USAIN BOLT SETS A NEW
100M SPRINT WORLD RECORD**

When: 16 August 2009

Where: World Athletics Championships, Berlin

What happened? Usain Bolt took the World Athletics Championships by storm, becoming the world's fastest man when he won the 100-metre race with a record-breaking time of 9.58 seconds.

What changed? The 100-metre sprint final was hyped up in the media as a showdown between the reigning world champion – Tyson Gay from the USA – and world record holder Usain Bolt, from Jamaica. The race captured the attention of people everywhere. Bolt pulled away early, leaving Gay and the rest of the competitors behind. He achieved a world record time and took the gold medal. Global news coverage meant the whole world celebrated Bolt's outstanding achievement, setting a new goal for others to aim for.

Showing us the power of determination

13 SAVED IN THAM LUANG CAVE RESCUE

When: 23 June – 10 July 2018

Where: Tham Luang, Chiang Rai Province, Thailand

What happened? 12 boys and their football coach became trapped inside a long and narrow cave deep within a mountain. They had been exploring the cave during the day, but water from heavy rains suddenly flooded the cave, leaving them isolated on a small shelf 4 kilometres from the entrance.

What changed? The boys' story spread rapidly on social media, and journalists and expert cave divers from around the world travelled to Thailand to report the news and help with the rescue effort. The news reports highlighted the boys' determination to survive and the rescuers' unflinching commitment to free them. It was an inspiring story of courage, community and resilience.

Making us question our history

PROTESTORS PULL DOWN STATUE OF SLAVE TRADER

When: 7 June 2020

Where: Bristol, UK

What happened? A group of protestors pulled down a statue of former Bristol citizen Edward Colston and pushed it into the river. Inspired by the Black Lives Matter protests in the USA, they targeted the statue of Colston because he had become rich by selling Black people as slaves in the 1600s.

What changed? Citizen journalism played an important role as clips of the statue being brought down spread on social media. The news sparked a national debate about how we celebrate people who were important in our history, but whose actions were unacceptable.

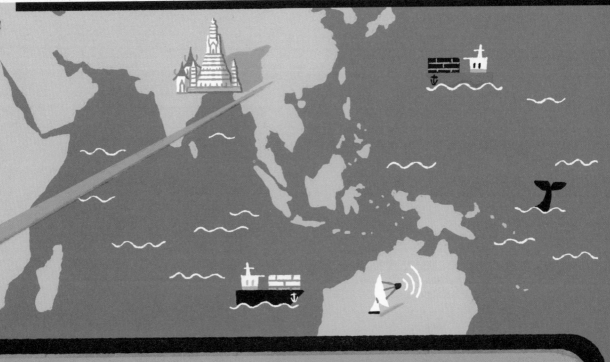

Protecting our values

STORMING OF THE CAPITOL

When: 6 January 2021

Where: The Capitol Building, Washington D.C., USA

What happened? After losing the 2020 United States presidential election, former President Donald Trump falsely told his supporters that the election had been rigged against him. On 6 January 2021, as Joe Biden was being confirmed as the new president, Donald Trump spoke to his supporters, urging them to challenge the outcome of the election. Angered by Trump's speech, a large gathering of his supporters broke into the building, vandalising property and terrorising those inside.

What changed? A team from ITV News in the UK was the only TV news crew in the building to film the trespassers' actions. Their reports showed the scale and violence of the attack as it happened, and they also questioned rioters in the moment about their motives. The shocking images and statements from the day showed just how important fact-checking is in order to protect people from the harmful effects of fake news.

LET'S GET DIGITAL

News online comes in lots of shapes and sizes. From in-depth analysis to snappy headlines to energetic explainers, entertaining podcasts, written articles, funny memes, random opinions, news that's super reliable or really quite dodgy – it's all out there! It might sound confusing but it's simple to navigate online news when it's broken down. First, let's look at something you might be more familiar with: a TV news organisation. Here's how it creates news for its online platforms.

Online news with strong roots

A TV news organisation produces all the content for its scheduled bulletins and online platforms from the same newsroom. This means that its online news – whether that's shorter versions of TV packages or original reports made for online platforms – is made to the same standard and sticks to the same rules as its TV counterpart.

WEBSITES
The online team creates blogs, podcasts and written articles that expand on the reports from the scheduled bulletin. They cover breaking news as well as stories that don't appear on TV.

SCHEDULED NEWS BULLETIN
Reports produced for scheduled TV news bulletins are made available to the reporters and producers who assemble content for the online platforms.

LONG-FORM VIDEO PLATFORMS
On these platforms, the news organisation's video content is sorted under different tabs. You can watch TV reports, reports made specifically for social media platforms and even live streams of important events and announcements.

IMAGE AND VIDEO SHARING PLATFORMS

These platforms post super-short versions of reports about issues and topics that are relevant to younger audiences, plus images that capture the headline stories of the day.

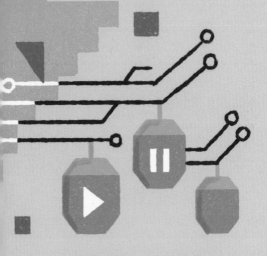

SHORT-FORM VIDEO PLATFORMS

Short explainers from the news organisation's reporters that unpack complicated stories work well on these types of platforms. The informal presenting style makes them feel authentic and they tackle topics in a way that appeals to the younger audiences that typically use these platforms.

Making news for websites

Websites are brilliant spaces for news because they're so flexible. They often feature a mix of written articles with strong, short headlines and video reports to go along with them, so you can choose whether to watch or read or both. They can be used to cover longer news stories that are packed with detail or breaking news as it happens.

When making news for websites, editors use some clever online-only features. When big events happen, they will blog the story live as it happens, giving instant updates. For other stories, editors will add links to specialist websites for people who want to find out more.

Making news for social media

If the digital editor thinks a TV report would interest audiences on social media, they'll create a short, edited version of it. They adapt the shape of the footage to fit the platform and add graphics and a logo so that audiences know which news organisation has created it. It's a skilled job to create clips that contain all the key information and remain fair. Often, three or four clips are bundled together and dropped at a specific time of day like straight after school – just like a mini bulletin.

Listen up

Podcasts are another type of online news. They focus on sound, not images – like radio for the digital age! A reporter might talk to expert guests about a long-running news story to share more views and information on that topic, a bit like a documentary or investigation. Other podcasts might have a host and a panel of people with different views on the stories they're analysing. This leads to sparky, entertaining debates that can help listeners form their own opinions.

What is online news?

Online is the go-to place for news for most people today, so I bet you know a bit about it already, like how TV or print news organisations have their own news websites, social media channels and podcasts. But that's not the only online news out there – lots of news organisations exist exclusively online, either as websites or video channels or blogs, and they range from big companies with hundreds of employees to a couple of people or even one person.

World Wide Web or wild wild west?

The internet doesn't have a regulator, which means that news websites don't have to follow the same rules as newspapers and TV news. But just because online news organisations aren't regulated, it doesn't automatically mean their news is less trustworthy. They may make up their own set of rules that they stick to when making reports, such as a commitment to being balanced or using multiple sources. We just need to be aware of what those rules or values are. And it's important to keep in mind that some may not follow any rules at all, so when you search for a news report online, it's a bit of a lucky dip!

Navigating news online

We can enjoy this treasure trove of reporting, but we have to use our analytical skills to identify what kind of news we're seeing. There are a couple of questions you can ask to work out if you can trust what you're reading or watching online.

OPINION OR FACT?

Opinion pieces are a key feature of news. They let us know what experts are thinking about a certain topic. Often they are clearly labelled online, but sometimes they're presented as fact. Try to spot if the story you're reading supports one particular point of view. If it does, then it's probably an opinion and not a balanced report.

WHERE DOES IT COME FROM?

If you're reading a report but can't see the name of the journalist or a reference to the news organisation that first posted the story, do a search to find out. That way you can work out what kind of news it is.

DOUBLE CHECK

If you're unsure about a report you've seen, go to a different news organisation that you know and trust to see if and how they're reporting the story. This is especially useful when people or organisations announce their own news direct to their followers.

NEWS ALERT
GOING VIRAL

It's so easy to share news on social media platforms – just a click of a button and it shoots off to all your followers. When a news story has been forwarded hundreds of times beyond its original audience, it's gone viral. At that point, there's no way to control who sees it, which makes it doubly important to find out if what you're sharing is reliable before passing it on.

Too crazy to be true?

Online news is filled with funny, outrageous and jaw-dropping clips. Bears climbing into cars are fun videos to watch, but checking to see if they're true can be a headache. No matter how harmless they appear, news organisations still have to be sure that clips are real before featuring them on their site or feed. Journalists use online tools and techniques to find out who created the content when and where, to make sure it's real. These are called verified clips and news organisations can use them in their feed knowing the footage is real and accurate.

CITIZEN JOURNALISM

It's hard to imagine life before smartphones existed, but they have only been around since the mid 2000s. Since then, they've totally transformed the way we communicate by suddenly giving everyone the ability to take, send and receive images and videos faster than ever before. The combination of this powerful technology with the creation of social media platforms that allow us to share content with the world, sparked a new type of reporting: citizen journalism.

NEWS ALERT
THE FIRST CITIZEN JOURNALISM WEBSITE

Founded in 2000, OhMyNews in South Korea was one of the first citizen journalism websites, as it only published content submitted by its users.

What is citizen journalism?

Citizen journalism describes ordinary people who report news stories they're witnessing. This usually happens before any professional journalists arrive at the scene. Imagine you are at a shopping centre when a famous pop star starts to perform unexpectedly. It's super exciting, but there are no journalists there to report it. You decide to film the performance and post it online using some powerful hashtags and there you go, you're a citizen journalist.

Citizen journalism has a serious role too. When people are in dangerous situations such as war, or challenging situations like undergoing treatment for an illness, they might film their own story to show the world what's happening.

Is citizen journalism always a good thing?

Although citizen journalists are an important part of the news system, they don't have to stick to the same rules as official news channels. Here's what you need to know about this type of reporting.

CITIZEN JOURNALISM IS USEFUL BECAUSE...

IT ALLOWS US TO GET NEWS FROM PLACES TOO DANGEROUS OR DIFFICULT FOR JOURNALISTS TO REPORT FROM

In 2010, there was a series of protests in North Africa and the Middle East called the Arab Spring. Some countries didn't allow journalists in to report what was happening, so footage shot by protesters gave people first-hand accounts of what they were experiencing.

IT DELIVERS BREAKING NEWS

When an unexpected event occurs, such as a crime, extreme weather or travel disruption, people on the scene can often be the ones to break the story before professional journalists get there.

IT PROVIDES US WITH GOOD QUALITY, IMPACTFUL PICTURES

Smartphone technology has advanced so much that some reporters choose to film on smartphones instead of larger cameras. Simple, in-the-moment footage from citizen journalists can capture real emotions and tell a story more powerfully than only using words.

WE SHOULD BE CAUTIOUS OF CITIZEN JOURNALISM BECAUSE...

IT MIGHT BE BIASED

A citizen journalist might have a specific viewpoint or opinion about the event they are filming, so you may have to look somewhere else to find other sides to the story.

IT MIGHT BE A HOAX

A citizen journalist could claim anything they post is breaking news, so viewers have to fact-check to make sure the footage is trustworthy and reliable.

IT MIGHT NOT BE LEGAL

Journalists are aware of the laws and regulations that affect the stories they cover, from getting permission to reuse footage to making sure every fact is correct. Citizen journalists might not have this knowledge or make these checks.

ASK ME ANYTHING

IF CITIZEN JOURNALISTS CAN REPORT NEWS, WHY DO WE NEED JOURNALISTS?

Creating an informed news report involves a big team of people with different skills. Every element is checked in detail to make sure it's correct, and journalists make sure it contains different viewpoints to be balanced. Citizen journalism is helpful, but we should remember that it tells only one side of the story.

WE ARE
THE NEWS

The purpose of the news is to report events that affect us, which means, basically, we are the news. Local and national news should hold a mirror up to the communities we live in, so everyone watching or reading sees their experiences reflected at them in the reports. It's one of the principles that helps editors choose which news reports to include in their content and makes sure we see a range of stories. It makes sense, then, that as our communities are constantly changing, the news needs to change too.

Reflecting our audience

The best way to ensure different experiences are considered in the news we make is to have people involved at every stage who come from a mix of backgrounds. Things like our gender, sexuality, race, religion and financial circumstances can change the way we see the world and what things we find important. Having a range of people involved in the process means different points of view will shape the news reports we read and watch, and hopefully everyone will feel informed and included.

How does this work in action? Well, let's imagine all the editors, reporters, producers and everyone else working for a local news organisation live in beach houses and love surfing. You might find a lot of their news reports are about beach houses or surfing because these things are important to them and are what they see in their everyday lives. But what about local people who live in tall apartments or houses in the town? Or people who like gaming or cycling, and everyone else in the community who relies on this news? If the news doesn't show their world, they're going to feel that this organisation is not for them.

ON ASSIGNMENT
WINDOWS AND MIRRORS

Now that you have an idea of what the news should be, why don't you carry out your own survey of news stories that are windows (allowing us to see into others' lives) and mirrors (reflecting our own lives)? Watch a TV bulletin and make a tally of the kinds of reports you see.

Bringing communities together

As well as reflecting our own lives, the news should also be a window to the world and provide us with an opportunity to put ourselves in someone else's shoes. International news is a powerful way to help us appreciate the successes and challenges people face in other parts of the world. For example, a news report on the impact of a natural disaster in one country can help people who don't live there to understand a situation they haven't experienced. It makes people who live a long way apart feel much closer. Through international news, we can learn about other people and cultures, realise our similarities and differences and build supportive communities.

Inspiring the next generation

Have you ever been so impressed by someone you've met or seen in the media that you wished to be just like them? Yes? Well, that just shows the importance of role models. It's natural to be inspired by people who do impressive things, but you might feel a stronger connection with them if you share some of the same characteristics, like how you look or where you come from. That's why it's so important for audiences to see newsreaders, reporters and experts from across society appearing on the news. If we can see ourselves making the news, it can help us believe that a career in news and reporting is open to us.

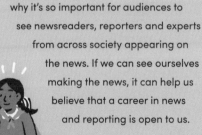

THE FUTURE OF NEWS

Technology has created a world where information can be spread in the blink of an eye, and there's no doubt that inventions we haven't yet dreamt of will create more dynamic ways for news to be made, delivered and consumed. These changes could have some amazing effects, but we also know from our timeline of news inventions that concerns about reliability date back to the very beginning. So let's look at what future tech could mean for news, and how we can best prepare ourselves for it.

Who's the editor?

Technology is central to how we get our news in more ways than you might think. On TV, in newspapers and on many news websites, living, breathing human editors decide which stories to feature. On social media platforms, a computer programme called an algorithm selects which stories appear in your feed. These algorithms are designed to learn which content we like and to show it to us continuously, encouraging us to stay on these platforms for longer.

What's the problem with that? Well, while real-life editors are concerned with delivering us a wide range of news, algorithms are not. Because these algorithms are only showing things you like, it becomes harder to discover new topics that might interest you, or important news. This means we have to be more aware about how and why news stories end up on our devices.

NEWS ALERT

ALGORITHMS

An algorithm is a set of instructions that a computer follows to solve problems or complete a task. On social media, algorithms are often designed to learn what you like to see based on your habits or likes, so it can fill your feed with more of the same content.

Echo-o-o-o chamber

Algorithms can also send posts to your feed that only reflect your own views back to you instead of challenging you with other points of view. When you're constantly surrounded by similar views to your own, you enter something called an 'echo chamber'. It's a bit like when you shout in a cave and hear your own voice bounce off the walls back to you. Like we've learned, hearing news featuring the views of different people allows us to understand our world better. In the future, as algorithms get more sophisticated, we will have to seek out news that offers multiple viewpoints more actively.

Artificial intelligence

Another big change in the way algorithms work is the development of artificial intelligence, or AI. AI has the ability to learn just like you can. But unlike a normal computer that relies on commands given by the user, AI is capable of making its own decisions. It can create images, text and other media using all the information available on the internet. This technology is very powerful and means we are going to have to be even more aware of who or what has created the news we consume.

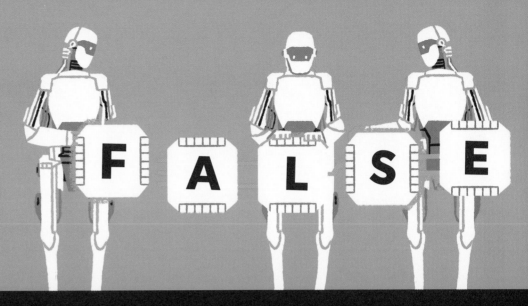

A helpful tool or a disruptive influence?

Lots of industries are looking at how AI can benefit them and news is no different. Currently, it's a fantastic tool for some tasks in the newsroom, such as helping reporters analyse huge amounts of information that would take humans a long time to process. On the flip side, AI can mislead people.

AI creates content using information from across the internet and, unlike human journalists, it doesn't ask whether each piece of information is real or true. When looking at AI-generated content, reporters have to check every fact against other sources to make sure the article, image or clip is reliable. Reporters also have to make sure that any information or images made by AI are being used with the owner's agreement and knowledge.

Another thing to keep in mind is that the information AI draws on is likely to contain the views of the people who created it. As a result, the content it generates may replicate particular viewpoints or stereotypes. This isn't helpful for journalists who want to include a diverse range of views in their work.

NEWS ALERT
DEEPFAKES

Deepfakes are videos that look real but have been manipulated to distort the original content to trick viewers into believing something that isn't true, like changing words people say, their background or clothing. Often, the changes are so good that they are difficult to spot, and this can be very misleading. If someone altered a news report in this way, it could have very harmful effects.

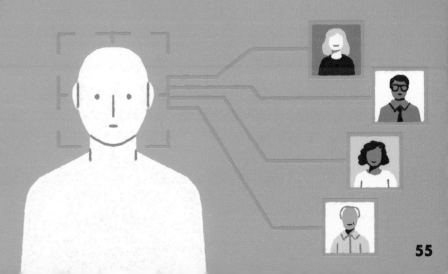

SO YOU WANT TO WORK IN NEWS?

Many of the jobs in the newsroom require similar skills, like being inquisitive, determined and being able to understand another person's point of view. But there's a big difference between being a camera operator and a programme editor. This quiz will help you find out which role might suit you.

1. You're at the front of the queue at the café. It's about to close and they need you to decide what you'd like quickly. You...

A. Buy your favourite cake and another you've never tried to see if you might like it better.

C. Choose the doughnut because you love them and know exactly what they're made of.

B. Ask the café owner what they would recommend.

D. Choose the pastry with the most eye-catching decoration.

2. Your friend asks if you want to see the latest blockbuster at the cinema. You...

A. Say yes, and go away to research the plot, director and actors beforehand.

C. Say you'll read more about the film first to check it's not too similar to the other shows you're watching.

B. Ask when and where it is and how you're getting there and back.

D. Jump at the chance to see awesome images on a big screen!

3. You're working on a project with a new piece of computer software but haven't been taught how to use it. You...

A. Do some digging yourself to find out if the software has advanced cool features and present what you've found to your class.

C. Download the guide, watch a tutorial and read reviews so you can find the best features that will be suited to your project.

B. Ask the teacher to give you a training session so you can find out the facts directly and also ask questions.

D. Are so excited you just dive in. You're a tech wizard, and who cares about making mistakes whilst figuring it out?! You'll be using it like a pro in an hour or so anyway!

4. You haven't been picked for a place in your school's sports team. It's upsetting, but do you...

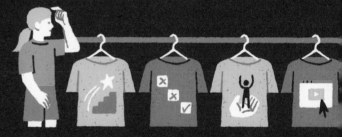

A. Resolve to make the team next time and be their star player.

C. Assist the coach so you can help the players who did make the team.

B. Ask the coach where you went wrong so you can improve.

D. Show your support by making a team website and editing together some awesome clips of them playing.

5. Choose a phrase that describes your best skills.

A. You're inquisitive and enjoy the limelight.

C. You're a good leader who sticks to the rules.

B. You have a thirst for knowledge and are good at organising things.

D. You're creative and have excellent attention to detail.

THE RESULTS!

MOSTLY As

Your answers suggest you have everything it takes to be a reporter – inquisitive, determined, analytical, confident and a clear communicator.

MOSTLY Bs

You would make a great producer! Producers enjoy organising things behind the scenes so that everything on screen is accurate, fair and engaging.

MOSTLY Cs

You are very balanced, don't make hasty decisions and are able to see the big picture. This means you'd make a great programme editor.

MOSTLY Ds

You have good technical skills, lots of creativity and the ability to work calmly under pressure. You're a camera operator or director for sure!

ON ASSIGNMENT
HOW MUCH DO YOU KNOW?

Now that you've learned the ins and outs of news, it's time to check out your skills. Complete these assignments to put your knowledge to the test and see if you can engage with the news like a top journalist.

Spotting fake news

Remember what we learned about fake news? If Nathan had checked the website that reported on exploding red bikes, he might have realised it was fake news. Now it's your turn to work out if a website is reporting reliable news. Read the story below and use the tips to decide whether the story is true or fake.

www.4Chanel_news1.co

By Chief Correspondent

HAMSTER RUNS FASTER THAN HUMAN

Disclaimer: All news articles on this website are made up. We write them to have a bit of fun and they're not to be taken seriously.

Today, Olympic sprint champion Federico was beaten in a 100m race by his pet hamster. Federico told our reporter: "This race was totally unfair! Helena has four legs whereas I only have two, and she was wearing performance-enhancing shoes on all four feet. I demand a rematch!"

1.
Look at the URL - the address of the website. Does it look like a normal URL that you would recognise, or is there something strange about it?

2.
Some websites exist with the purpose of making up stories that poke fun at real news. Usually, these websites clearly declare that the stories they post are false so people don't confuse them with real news. Is there is a note on this website?

3.
Who wrote the story? Is there a named reporter you can search for online? If it's a real reporter with some experience, a search should bring up a list of reports they have written.

4.
Does the news story sound strange, shocking or too good to be true? If so, check to see if other trusted news sites are reporting the same thing.

5.
Check the images. Sometimes fake news stories use real pictures from an unrelated story to make their report look legitimate.